LIGHT WAVES

BY DAVID A. ADLER

ILLUSTRATED BY ANNA RAFF

Holiday House New York

For Sophie, Ethan, Zach, Jared, Elliott, and their dog, Bodhi. —D. A. A.

For Kay and Marianna. —A. R.

The publisher wishes to thank Dr. Albert Rigosi of the National
Institute of Standards and Technology for his expert review of the text.

HOLIDAY HOUSE is registered in the U.S. Patent and Trademark Office.
Printed and Bound in December 2017 at Tien Wah Press in Johor Bahru, Malaysia.
The artwork was created digitally.
www.holidayhouse.com
First Edition
1 3 5 7 9 10 8 6 4 2

Library of Congress Cataloging-in-Publication Data
Names: Adler, David A., author. | Raff, Anna, illustrator.
Title: Light waves / David A. Adler ; illustrated by Anna Raff.
Description: First edition. | New York : Holiday House, [2018] | Audience: 6–10
Identifiers: LCCN 2017006616 | ISBN 9780823436828 (hardcover) | ISBN 0823436829 (hardcover)
Subjects: LCSH: Light–Juvenile literature.
Classification: LCC QC360 .A27 2018 | DDC 535 dc23 LC record available at https://lccn.loc.gov/2017006616

We need light to see.

Plants need light to grow. Animals need plants to eat.

Since plants and animals are the food we eat, we would have no food without light.

Without light we just could not survive.

We need *light*, but what is it? You can see it but you can't touch it. You can't hold it, carry it, taste it, or smell it. Light is a form of *energy*. Energy is the ability to do work.

Energy comes from the sun in the form of sunlight.

It is transferred to the grass, then to the cattle.

4

You can't make energy. You can't destroy it. Energy can only be transferred—moved—from one thing to another. For example, sunlight is a form of energy. It helps grass grow. Cows eat grass, and the grass they eat helps them grow. Later, meat from these cows is used to make hot dogs. Even later, people get energy from eating those hot dogs.

From the cattle it is transferred to the hot dogs.

From the hot dogs it is transferred to us.

Much of our light comes from the sun. Light from the sun, *solar energy*, can be collected. It can be used to power our machines and heat our homes.

The sun is almost 93 million miles, or about 150 million kilometers, from Earth. That's a long way. It would take a car speeding at 60 miles, or about 97 kilometers, an hour more than 170 years to travel that far. But it takes sunlight just eight minutes to travel from the sun to Earth. Light travels at the tremendous speed of 186,282 miles per second, or 299,792 kilometers per second.

That's fast! Nothing travels faster.

When we see light we're seeing streams of light waves. These streams are made of *photons*. Photons are tiny bits of light that travel together in wavy streams of light.

You can think of the waves as very long bands with crests—high points—and valleys—low points. Waves of light, with their crests and valleys, travel in straight lines.

Let's show that light waves travel in straight lines.

What you will need:

flashlight

book

2 cardboard tubes from rolls of toilet paper or paper towels

tape

1. Stand the book up on a desk or table with the front facing you.

2. Hold the flashlight close to the book, and turn it on. The front of the book is bathed in light. The back is not. That's because light waves travel in straight lines. They travel straight at the book. They do not go around it.

3. Next, tape the two cardboard tubes together. You now have one long tube.

4. Take the tubes and flashlight to someplace dark. Shine the flashlight through one end of the tube. The light should shine through the tube and out the other end.

5. Now, where the two tubes are taped, bend them so they no longer form one straight tube.

6. Shine the flashlight through one end of the tube. The light waves will not shine through the other end because light waves only travel in straight lines.

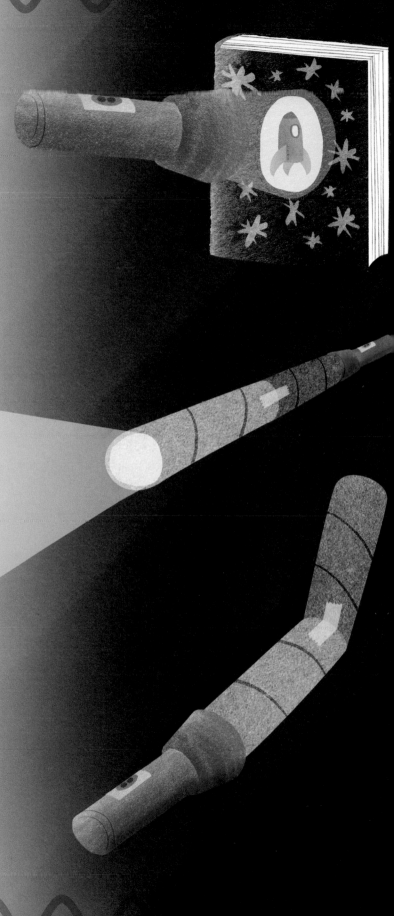

Light waves travel through air in straight lines. But you can bend light.

Let's bend light waves.

What you will need:
a clear glass
a drinking straw

Fill the glass at least halfway with water. Put the straw in the water. The straw seems to bend at the waterline.

The straw looks bent, but it's not. Take the straw out of the water. It's straight. The straw seemed to bend when it was in the water because light waves travel more slowly through water than through air.

When light waves travel at different speeds they seem to bend things. This is called *refraction*.

Light won't travel at all through this book. It doesn't travel through stone or wood. It won't travel through you. Stone, wood, books, and people are opaque. Light won't pass through them.

Opaque objects and light rays form *shadows*.

Let's create shadows.

What you will need:
toy blocks
flashlight
a room that can be darkened

On the floor or on a table, pile the blocks into a tower. Darken the room. Turn on the flashlight and point its light at the blocks.

One side of the tower is bathed in light. You can see the blocks clearly. Look directly behind the blocks. There's a dark shape on the floor or table. It's roughly the same shape as the tower of blocks. That darkened shape is a shadow. Shadows are formed when opaque objects block light rays.

Light does travel through some things.
Of course, light travels through air. Light also travels through glass and clear plastic wrap. That's because air, glass, and clear plastic wrap are *transparent*.

Light doesn't travel completely through wax paper, frosted glass, or honey. If you look through a sheet of wax paper, whatever is on the other side of the paper seems blurry. That's because wax paper, frosted glass, and honey are *translucent*.

Light waves bounce off surfaces such as apples, the hoods of cars, and large bodies of water. When light waves hit a shiny and completely flat surface, the light waves bounce straight back. Then, you get a *reflection* of what is facing that shiny flat surface.

A mirror is shiny and flat. It reflects just about all the light that hits it. The light bounces directly off the mirror so you get an almost perfect reflection of whatever is facing it.

Imagine you're in a playground and you throw a ball against a wall. The ball bounces right back. That's what happens when you look at a mirror. The light waves bounce right back.

When you look at a surface that's not as shiny and flat as a mirror the light rays don't bounce right back. They become somewhat scattered so you don't get an exact reflection.

Get a large, shiny metal soupspoon. It's shiny like a mirror but it's not flat.

Look at the back of the spoon. You can see yourself, but it's not an exact reflection. Your reflection should be somewhat elongated.

19

To understand why your reflection is elongated, imagine you are in a playground with a huge half-globe. If you throw the ball against the top part of the globe the ball bounces up.

If you throw the ball straight ahead it bounces straight back.

If you throw the ball against the bottom part of the globe the ball bounces down.

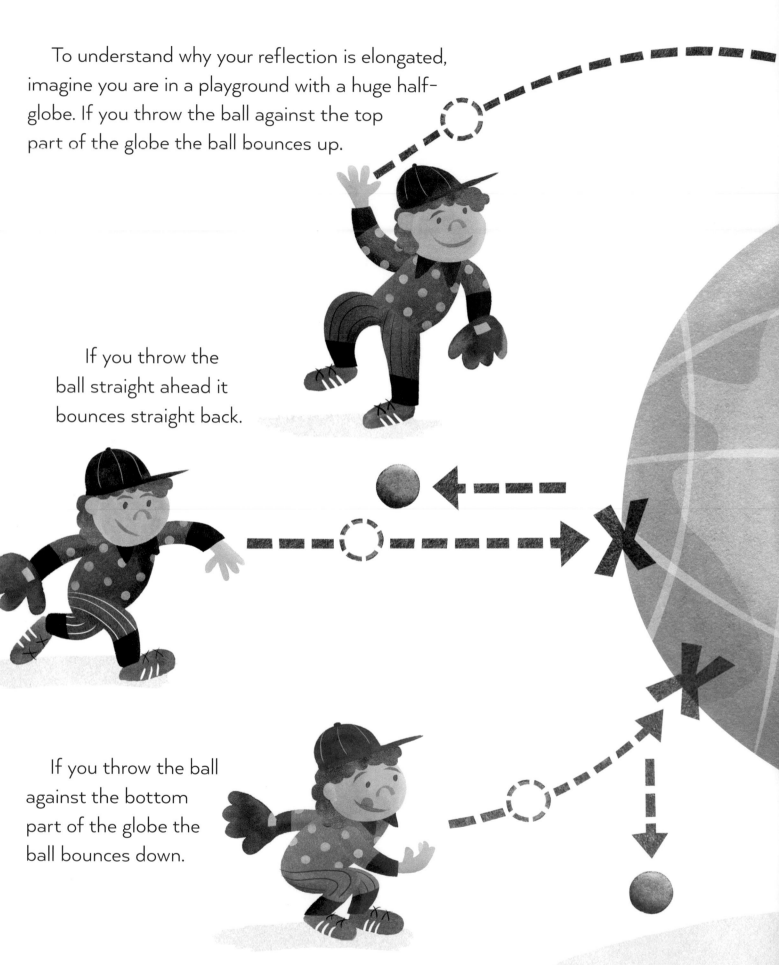

That's what happens when you look at the back of the spoon. The light waves do not all bounce straight back. Light waves bounce up off the top of the spoon and down off the bottom.

Look at the inside shiny bowl of the spoon, the side that scoops up soup. Your reflection is upside down.

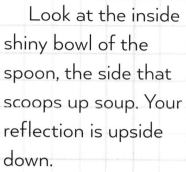

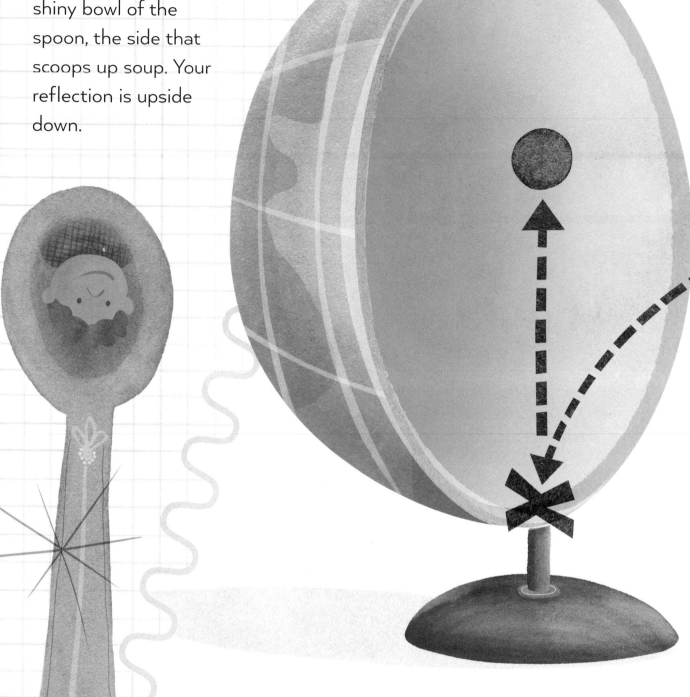

To understand why your reflection is upside down, imagine you walk behind the huge half-globe in the playground and there's no back to it. It's a large concave shape.

If you throw the ball down against the bottom part of the globe the ball bounces up.

When you look at the front of the spoon, light waves that strike the bottom of the spoon bounce up, and light waves that strike the top of the spoon bounce down.

up

down

Up goes down and down goes up! The reflection on a shiny concave shape is upside down.

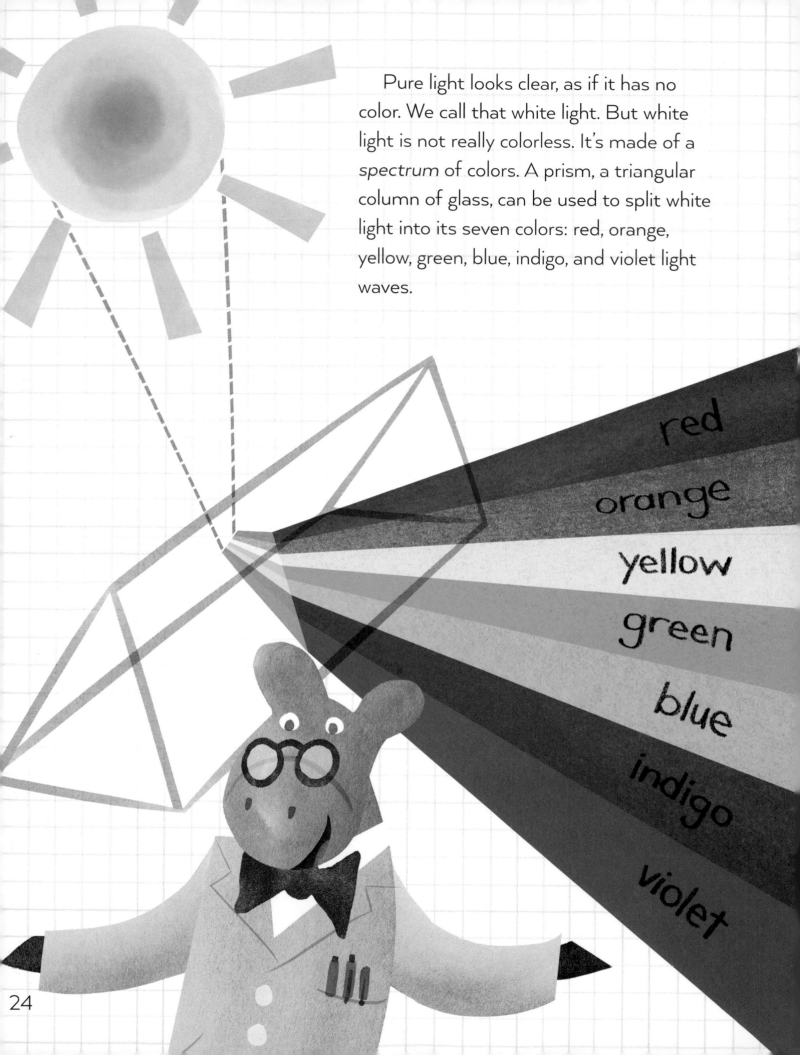

Pure light looks clear, as if it has no color. We call that white light. But white light is not really colorless. It's made of a *spectrum* of colors. A prism, a triangular column of glass, can be used to split white light into its seven colors: red, orange, yellow, green, blue, indigo, and violet light waves.

red

orange

yellow

green

blue

indigo

violet

24

Think again of light waves as wavy bands made up of tiny bits of light. These bands of light have crests (high points) and valleys (low points).

What makes the colors of the light waves different is the distance each color has between its crests. With the red waves the distance between the crests is greatest.

The distance is smallest with the violet waves.

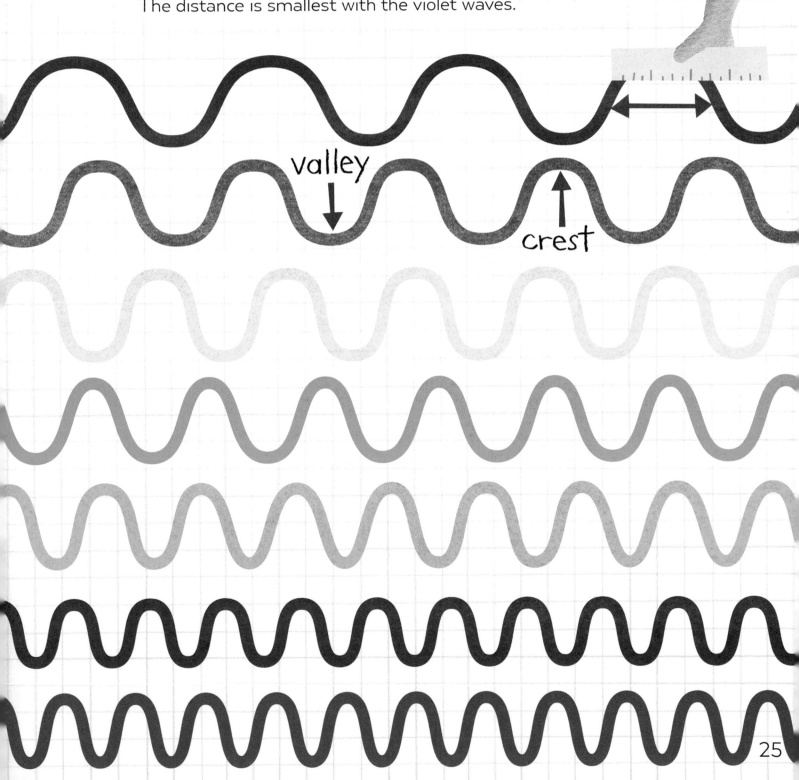

valley

crest

We see objects because light waves are reflected off them. But not all light waves are reflected. Some light waves are absorbed.

When an apple appears red it's because red light waves are reflected off the apple. The other colored waves are absorbed.

red

When a sheet of paper appears white all the colors of the spectrum are reflected off the paper.

When the cover of your notebook appears black none of the colors of the spectrum are reflected. They have all been absorbed.

Light does more than *illuminate* our world. It colors it.

white

black

Light waves are just part of the electromagnetic spectrum, the visible part of waves of energy that pass through our world.

In the visible spectrum the distance between the crests of the waves is greatest with red light. But there are light waves with a slightly greater distance between crests. We just cannot see them. Those are *infrared* light waves, sometimes called *hot light*.

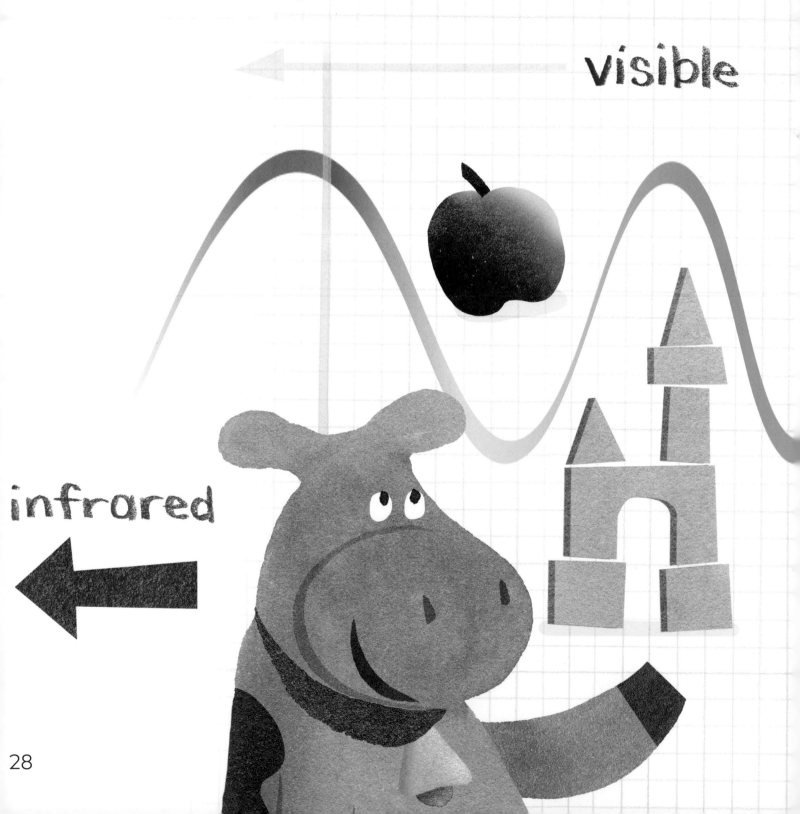

visible

infrared

In the visible spectrum the distance between the crests of the waves is smallest with violet light. But there are light waves with a slightly shorter distance between crests. We just cannot see them. Those are *ultraviolet* light waves, a form of radiation that gives us suntans.

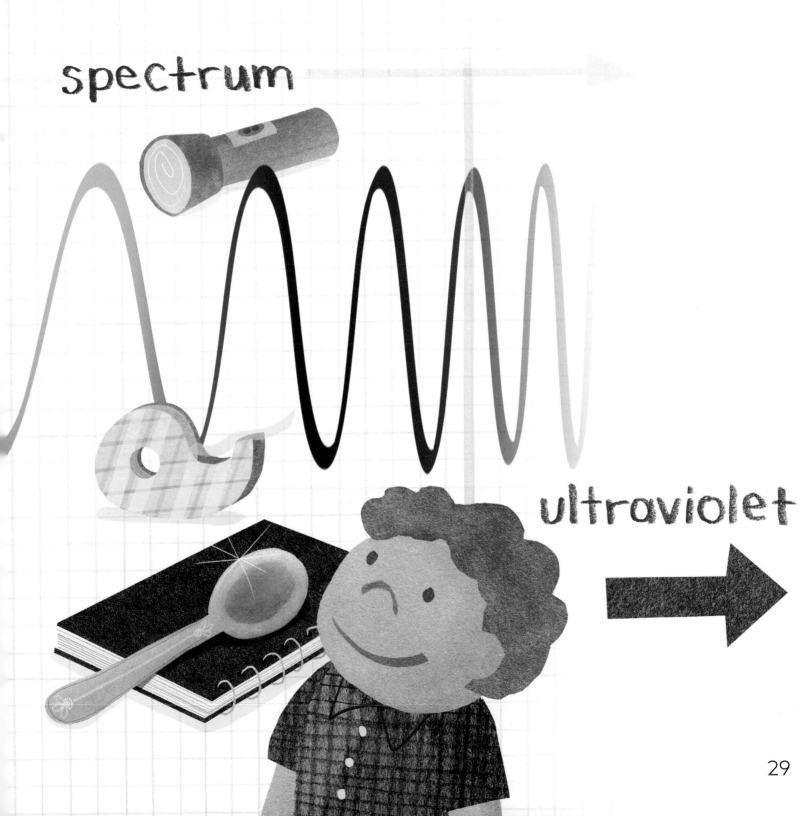

spectrum

ultraviolet

radio waves

microwaves

gamma rays

X-rays

In addition to ultraviolet and infared waves that we cannot see, there are other waves of energy beyond the visible spectrum, including *microwaves*, *radio waves*, *X-rays*, and *gamma rays*.

There's certainly more to the form of energy we know as light than simply flicking a switch and illuminating a dark room. Light sustains our world.

INDEX / GLOSSARY

energy—the ability to do work

gamma rays—dangerous rays on the invisible part of the electromagnetic spectrum
with various uses including killing cancer cells

illuminate—light up, brighten

infrared—rays on the invisible part of the electromagnetic spectrum that we feel as heat

light—the form of energy that enables us to see things and plants to grow

light waves—streams of photons that travel together

microwaves—rays on the invisible part of the electromagnetic spectrum used in cooking and radar

opaque—does not let light through

photons—tiny bits of light

prism—a triangular column of glass that can split white light into colors

radio waves—rays on the invisible part of the electromagnetic spectrum used to transmit sound

reflection—light waves bouncing off a surface

refraction—light waves bending as they pass through one medium to another,
for example, from air to water

shadow—dark area formed when an opaque object blocks light rays

solar energy—energy collected from sunlight

spectrum—the band of colors that make up light

translucent—when an object allows light waves to partially pass through

transparent—when an object allows light waves to fully pass through, and we can see through it

ultraviolet light—rays on the electromagnetic spectrum invisible to us
but visible to some insects and animals

X-rays—rays on the invisible part of
the electromagnetic spectrum that go
through many solid materials, leading to
their use in medicine and security